Original title:
A Balcony of Bliss

Copyright © 2025 Creative Arts Management OÜ
All rights reserved.

Author: Beckett Sinclair
ISBN HARDBACK: 978-1-80581-916-5
ISBN PAPERBACK: 978-1-80581-443-6
ISBN EBOOK: 978-1-80581-916-5

What Lies Beyond the Parapet

Up high I sit with snacks galore,
Watching the world, oh what a chore!
Socks on the line, they wave and dance,
While neighbors below take a second glance.

Birds calm my worries, or so I thought,
Until they bombed my head with a spot!
I laugh and curse, it's quite a scene,
This rooftop circus, my very own queen.

Sipping lemonade, my fancy drink,
Waving to strangers, what do they think?
A jester here, on my lofty throne,
Crafting a jest, not feeling alone.

As clouds roll by, they giggle and tease,
My dreams take flight, carried by breeze.
What lies beyond? A giggling spree,
My life's a comedy, come share with me!

The Edge of Tranquility

On the edge of my seat, I sit with glee,
My neighbor's cat thinks it's a tree.
With a cup of tea, I watch the show,
As squirrels play chess in a row.

A bee buzzes past, I give it a glare,
It lands in my hair, quite the affair!
I'm a laughing stock, perched high above,
In my haven of joy, I feel the love.

Views Beyond the Gloom

Peeking through curtains, I see the strife,
A jogger trips, oh, what a life!
With a laugh, I sip my lemonade,
While clouds hold a grumpy parade.

Birds sing off-key, oh, how they squawk,
Mixing the rhythm of my balcony talk.
Each gaffe and guffaw brings pure delight,
In the chaos, I find my flight.

A Retreat from the Noise

In my cozy corner, the world gets loud,
But I'm entertained by a passing crowd.
A dog in a tutu, what a sight,
I chuckle and grin, all feels right.

Thunderstorms rage, as I sip my drink,
A puddle of laughter, oh, don't you think?
Umbrellas collide like a rainy dance,
I cheer for the chaos; it's my romance.

Serenity's Secret Nook

In this secret spot, the world's a stage,
Where goofy antics trivialize rage.
I spot a pigeon wearing a hat,
I can't help but laugh at this quiz of a cat.

The neighbor's dog joins; he's got style,
Chasing his tail, now that's worthwhile!
With chuckles and smiles, I soak it all in,
Serenity's antics make the fun begin.

Nectar of the Daydream

Sipping sunlight from a cup,
I swear it's made of daisies.
My neighbor's cat is climbing up,
While I'm lost in summer hazes.

Clouds wear hats, oh what a show,
Dancing in the gentle breeze.
A laugh occurs, the winds they blow,
As butterflies steal all my cheese.

Elevated Whispers

Perched up high I spy on life,
The squirrels are plotting mischief.
One's about to steal my strife,
While birds preen like a show-off tiff.

The daisies gossip, so I lean,
Caught in their chatter and delight.
A teacup joins, what a routine,
As we sip giggles into night.

Tranquil Skies Await

Clouds drape like a cozy quilt,
As I lounge with berries ripe.
My chair now thinks it's built of gilt,
Woken by a giggling hype.

Watching ants dance like they're stars,
They surely have a secret plan.
Might I join, or stay with jars?
In this retreat, I am the man.

The Horizon's Invitation

The sun bows down, a silly prank,
As shadows slip from sturdy trees.
Inviting me to join the flank,
While I dance with the subtle breeze.

Oh the joy in this grand affair,
My flip-flops are rebels, truly.
They skip and hop without a care,
As daylight fades and acts unruly.

Celestial Conversations

Beneath the stars, I chat with cats,
They laugh at me, wearing little hats.
The moon winks, my secrets they keep,
While squirrels plot their heist in sleep.

Planets roll their eyes at my jokes,
While comets giggle as they poke.
Galaxies swirl, what a cosmic tease,
I swear they snicker at my sneezes.

Nature's Loving Gaze

The flowers gossip, oh what a scene,
Daisies dance in spots of green.
Trees share whispers, soft and sweet,
While bees do cha-cha on happy feet.

A butterfly giggles, flutters in glee,
As grasshoppers sing, 'Come dance with me!'
Nature's orchestra plays my favorite tune,
A symphony led by the curious moon.

A Sojourn in Stillness

I sit in quiet, but squirrels shout,
'Hey, human! Come join this roundabout!'
Leaves rustle softly, a wind-blown cheer,
While lazy clouds just giggle near.

Time drips like honey, I'm glued to the spot,
Sipping sunlight, oh, like it or not!
Moments stretch, teasing with delight,
Who knew stillness could spark such a flight?

Cloud Nine Chronicles

On fluffy puffs, I float and dream,
While drizzles fall like a splashy theme.
Joy rides along with a giggle and swoosh,
Rainbow cheers in a fanciful whoosh.

Frogs in bow ties join the parade,
With each croak, more laughter's made.
As sunbeams frolic and shadows play,
Life is a laugh, come what may!

Where the Sky Meets the Heart

Up high I sit, with tea in hand,
Watching the world, it's quite unplanned.
The squirrels dance, they steal my snack,
I swear they conspire, planning their attack.

Birds chirp loud, they think they're cool,
While I'm just here, my own little fool.
A breeze blows by, it messes my hair,
I laugh at the chaos, with nothing to care.

Clouds float by, in shapes so grand,
I point and giggle, it's all quite bland.
A dragon! A snail! They're all in my sight,
Just me and my thoughts, under the light.

As dusk approaches, the stars shine bright,
I toast to the night, what a silly flight.
With laughter and joy, it feels just right,
In this hidden space, my heart takes flight.

Songs of the Open Air

Up here above, the birds sing tunes,
While I just hum, like a misplaced goon.
The world below, in a dizzy whirl,
I drop some crumbs, watch the chaos unfurl.

A pigeon lands, thinks it's a star,
Waddling over, like it knows who you are.
It struts and prances, so proud and vain,
I can't help but laugh at its silly gain.

Leaves rustle soft, with stories to tell,
Of giggling cats, and where they fell.
The clouds morph shapes, a show for the bold,
I cheer them on, as their brilliance unfolds.

The sun gives a wink, dips out of view,
I wave goodbye, feeling light and new.
From my perch above, the world's a big joke,
Here on my spot, I giggle and poke.

Resting Place of Reflection

Here I lounge, feet dangling down,
The world looks foolish, a circus clown.
Thoughts bounce around, like a rubber ball,
In this sweet spot, I embrace it all.

With a mix of sun, and a splash of shade,
The day's little quirks, I can't evade.
A neighbor shouts, but I can't hear,
I'm lost in laughter, feeling no fear.

A cat strolls by, so regal and fine,
I wonder, does it sip on good wine?
With every pounce, it claims its throne,
While I just chuckle, here all alone.

As the evening falls, and crickets sing,
In my elevated nook, oh what joy they bring.
With every note, my heart takes flight,
In this resting place, everything's right.

Leisure Above the Crowds

Here in my spot, away from the fuss,
The city below, a chaotic bus.
I sip my drink, watch the people chase,
While I relish this serene little space.

A child with balloons floats right on by,
They rise and rise, almost touch the sky.
I can't help but grin at their gleeful flight,
While I lounge here, feeling just right.

Neighbors argue, a dog starts to bark,
I chuckle softly, living in the lark.
Every little sound, a whimsical tune,
As laughter dances beneath the moon.

With stars above, and my heart aglow,
I toast to the night, the wild and the slow.
From my lofty perch, the world's a delight,
In my little haven, everything's bright.

Floating on Gentle Thoughts

On a shelf of dreams, I lie,
With a sandwich and the sky.
My cat's plotting to take a nap,
While I eat crumbs, oh what a crap!

Clouds are chairs, and I recline,
In a fantasy, I'll soon dine.
The sun tickles my lazy head,
While ants march past, I'm not yet dead!

A breeze whispers jokes in my ear,
I laugh so hard, the squirrels cheer.
Life is breezy, like my toast,
But I think I like the jam the most!

So here I am, just floating by,
With a smile that's wider than the sky.
In this silly, cushy space,
I find joy in every trace.

Rays of Golden Calm

Sunshine spills like melted cheese,
Warming toes with playful ease.
I dance with shadows, don't you see?
They're quite the fun crowd, just like me!

A flower waves, it's feeling bold,
While butterflies trade secrets untold.
Lemonade laughs, sweet and bright,
In this golden slice of delight.

The grass tickles my toes, I squeal,
Bouncing like a rubber wheel.
A bird chirps puns up in the trees,
While ants form lines like they're at ease.

In this sunny, silly parade,
Life's an ice cream that won't fade.
Rays of joy spill everywhere,
Cheese, sunshine, and breezy air!

Conversations with Shadows

My shadow's got a joke to share,
We giggle softly without a care.
It tells stories of my silly feet,
A dance-off with squirrels, oh what a treat!

We chat about clouds and strange dreams,
About flying pies and whipped cream streams.
It whispers secrets of the night,
While I try to hold in my delight.

The sun's retreating, but we're still here,
Plotting adventures, cracking good cheer.
A game of tag, we dash away,
As fireflies join in the play!

So here's to shadows, full of mirth,
Who make each moment feel like worth.
With a wink and a cheeky jest,
They remind me life's a playful quest!

The Sky's Soft Embrace

Up high, where the giggles float,
Clouds tickle me like a small boat.
I dream of riding a comet's tail,
To join the stars in a fun-filled sail.

The moon winks with a sly little grin,
It knows all the chaos that brews within.
Jupiter offers me cake and tea,
While Mars spins jokes, oh how they please!

A sprinkle of stardust, let's throw it about,
While laughter echoes in the cosmic rout.
Saturn's rings play catch with my hair,
In this playful realm, I've not a care.

So here I sway in infinity's hug,
Chasing dreams and giving the stars a shrug.
In the vast cosmos, I find my place,
With giggles shared in the sky's soft embrace.

Enclave of Infinite Calm

Upon my ledge, I see the world,
With coffee brewed, and bedhead unfurled.
The cat in charge, with regal flair,
She rules my heart from her plush chair.

The neighbors argue, yet I just grin,
They've lost the plot, where do I begin?
A seagull swoops, steals my pastry plate,
Oh blissful life, is this truly fate?

The skies may rumble, storms may yell,
But here with snacks, I know it well.
A dance of shadows, the sun dips low,
In my realm of giggles, I steal the show.

With books and snacks, my inner sage,
I twirl and twist like a daring mage.
So here I sit, with joy unbound,
In my corner, happiness is found.

Starlit Oasis

Under sparkly skies, I recline so sweet,
Counting stars while tapping my feet.
A comet rushes, I hear it say,
'Wish for pizza - and maybe a play!'

The moon stands guard, with a wink and cheer,
A serenade of crickets lends its ear.
Laughter bubbles, as I sip my drink,
What's life without a whimsical wink?

A raccoon scuttles, my snack's in sight,
Who knew this evening promised such delight?
With poetic musings and dreams upfront,
I drift in starlit laughter, truly a hunt.

The universe dances, the cosmos laughs,
With comic strips pinned like silly dafts.
Among these wonders, I twirl and sway,
In this joyful night, I must say, hooray!

Retreat of the Contented

In my nook of bliss, mischief flows,
I watch the world through a curtain's pose.
A squirrel steals my sandwich, I just sigh,
They say the grass is greener - you're telling a lie!

The radio crackles with tunes so bright,
I belt out notes in sheer delight.
Neighbors peek out, they raise an eyebrow,
But my shaky dance? Oh, what a wow!

Cats lounge around, plotting their schemes,
While I pursue the sweetest of dreams.
Why worry, when the night's full of cheer?
In this quirky haven, I hold it dear.

With frothy drinks and friends nearby,
I wave to stars and watch time fly.
Contentment reigns in giggles and glee,
In my happy retreat, I can just be me.

Rays of Dawn's Embrace

Sunrise spills like marmalade on toast,
Kicking off the day, a breakfast boast.
With sleepy yawns and socks mismatched,
I toast to joys, freshly hatched!

The dog runs amok, chasing his tail,
While I sip tea and tell a tall tale.
A roast in the oven, oh what a cinch,
Who knew my mornings could be such a pinch?

With laughter ringing across the warm glow,
I revel in silliness; it's my own show.
The sun rises higher, painting the skies,
With colors so lively, it fuels my highs.

So here I bask, as the day breaks free,
In moments of fun, just me and me.
With grins and giggles, the world I embrace,
In the rays of dawn's shimmer, I find my place.

Embracing the Horizon

A cat on the ledge, with a view so grand,
Waves at the pigeons, proclaims he's the man.
The seagulls just laugh, as they swoop and dive,
While he plots his escape, from this life to thrive.

In the sun, he does nap, on a warm, sunny tile,
Dreaming of tuna, just staying awhile.
A sip from the cup of the neighbor's cold brew,
Thinking, 'Life's pretty fine, when you're fuzzy and blue.'

Rapture on the Ridge

With a view so divine, and a hat on my head,
I sip my hot cocoa, in a deck chair I spread.
The wind plays a trick, it's a pirate's delight,
As marshmallows soar like they've taken to flight.

My buddy, the squirrel, has a stash of his gold,
He cackles and dances, feeling brave and bold.
While I clutch my mug and start twitching with glee,
'Next time, I'll bring snacks, you'll just wait and see!'

Solace Under Starlight

Under stars that are twinkling, what a sight to behold,
A raccoon comes to judge, like a critic so bold.
With popcorn in hand, I watch him critique,
My movie choice stinks, he gives me a peek!

'You call that a flick? You're completely misled!'
He munches my snacks, and he shakes his fat head.
Yet I laugh at his jest, in the warm summer night,
As he snuggles beside me and steals my last bite.

The Edge of Enlightenment

On the edge of the world, where wisdom might show,
I ponder the secrets only pros seem to know.
The wind comically shouts, 'You're a know-it-all fool!'
While a butterfly giggles, defying my rule.

I've placed my bold bets on the wisdom of crows,
But their advice feels like picking a bag filled with snow.
As I linger in confusion, a gust gives me flight,
'Thanks for the boost, now I soar like a kite!'

A Haven of Harmony

On a perch above the street,
I sip my tea, it's quite a feat.
Cats parade in little hats,
While pigeons gossip, where's the snacks?

Neighbors waving up so high,
Their laundry dancing in the sky.
I shout hello—then duck, oh dear!
And pause to laugh at their sleek rear.

A squirrel stops, gives me a wink,
As if he knows just what I think.
A hidden world, my keen delight,
Where chaos mingles with the light.

Where Time Suspends

Sipping coffee, time stands still,
A passing dog, a distant shrill.
I wave at clouds, they wave right back,
Imagining a cosmic snack.

One shoe drops from above my head,
The latest gossip, full of dread.
An opera singer lost in thought,
With a broom for a mic, oh, what a shot!

I jot it down, a silly scene,
As the sun dips low, a golden sheen.
Time's no rush—it's quite the fun,
When laughter rules, and moods are spun.

A Dance with the Wind

I sway along with breezy tunes,
While sunflowers high give me the goons.
A butterfly whirls in a twist,
Wouldn't mind if I added to the list!

The wind does jig, it loves to tease,
Tickling hair, it's such a breeze.
I try to cha-cha, feel a twirl,
And trip on my own unruly curl!

Neighbors peek from their cozy nooks,
Their faces painted with funny looks.
With laughter shared, we all take flight,
In a whirl of giggles, all feels right.

Reflections from the Summit

From up so high, the world's a game,
Each car below, a toy in fame.
I spy my friends with snacks galore,
Who knew climbing brought this score?

Echoes of laughter fill the air,
While birds play tag, without a care.
I wave at clouds, what a silly plot,
As they gather round, oh what a lot!

Reflections shine, a comical view,
As even the sun can't help but coo.
With every chuckle, hearts align,
On this peak, the world's divine!

Freedom's Lullaby

Up high I sit, with snacks in tow,
The world below moves nice and slow.
Birds fly by with gossip to share,
In this grand escape, I haven't a care.

My neighbors wave, looking quite absurd,
Wearing pajamas, not a single word.
Sipping their tea, they chuckle and grin,
As I ponder if I should dive in.

The cat thinks I'm quite the odd sight,
Flopping like a fish, chasing its flight.
Laughing, I dance, though no one can see,
Freedom's a joy, just kidding, it's me!

As day turns to dusk, the laughs never cease,
Each moment outside is a moment of peace.
I'll stay on my perch, with dreams in my mind,
Wishing for clouds that're fluffy and kind.

Landing on Soft Clouds

With arms spread wide, I leap from the edge,
Thinking I'll float like a soft feathered pledge.
The ground rushes up, I scream like a bird,
Landing on cushions—oh wait, that's absurd!

A trampoline bounces, my day gets more wild,
Flipping and flopping like a giddy child.
I wave at the sky with a giggle and cheer,
While the pigeons below just stare and sneer.

Ticklish breezes wrap round my toes,
Swaying to music that nobody knows.
I'm lost in my laughter, I'm drifting away,
The clouds are my buddies, they're here for the play.

A sky full of whimsy, no worries in sight,
I'll dance with the raindrops till day turns to night.
As I float on my laughter, my heart takes a bow,
Floating through life, landing soft on a cloud.

Reveries at Dusk

As daylight fades, the giggles grow loud,
Silly creatures gather, both lively and proud.
The moon winks at stars, they break into song,
In this twilight ballet, I feel I belong.

Fireflies twinkle like stars who got lost,
Dancing around me, no matter the cost.
Grinning with mischief, the shadows take flight,
Here in my reverie, all feels just right.

Twirling and swirling, I spin like a top,
In blissful abandon, I can't help but hop.
The world may be quirky, but so am I,
With laughter and dreams, we'll reach for the sky.

So bring on the dusk with its magic and mirth,
In this twilight wonder, I've found my birth.
With giggles as whispers, I'll dance until dawn,
In reveries of joy, I'm blissfully drawn.

Voice of the Gentle Breeze

The breeze tickles my nose, a cheeky tease,
It whispers sweet secrets, with flair and ease.
Twirling the curtains, painting the day,
While I chase after thoughts that have run away.

A gust plays a tune, a raucous delight,
Bumps into my hat, takes off in its height.
I leap in pursuit, with a giggle or two,
Chasing down whispers, oh, what will they do?

It dances through flowers, sending them spinning,
Local bees buzzing, ready for winning.
Though I may stumble, my laughter won't cease,
With each breeze-tinged note, I feel light and free.

So let's sway with the air, let giggles ascend,
In the voice of the breeze, where laughter won't end.
I'm lost in the moments, the fun revelry,
In a world full of wonder, come dance with me!

Embracing the Atmosphere

Up on high, I jiggle and sway,
Feathers dance on a breezy day.
Birds gossip loud, chirp, and tease,
While I sip lemonade with ease.

My neighbor's cat is caught in a sunbeam,
Pretending to chase after a dream.
A passing dog gives a curious glance,
As I break into a silly dance.

Laughing clouds float with great delight,
Juggling sunshine, pure and bright.
With friends of the wind, I spin and twirl,
In this sky-high, giggling whirl.

So, come join me, let joy take flight,
We'll toast to antics and pure delight.
Embracing all, in playful jest,
This life we live is simply the best.

Petals of Peace

Frogs in tuxedos croak in style,
Dressed to impress with a goofy smile.
Dandelions float like wishful dreams,
While I roll in petals, laughter beams.

Bumblebees buzz like they've got a plan,
While I chase them, feeling like a fan.
With flowers chatting in fragrant tones,
I lost my shoe, and so my phone!

The breeze brings whispers of silly lore,
Like fashion tips from a friendly floor.
A butterfly flutters, winks at me,
Saying, "Dance like no one can see!"

Underneath the sun's bright embrace,
Nonsense reigns in this vibrant space.
Among petals of peace, fun is the key,
In this garden, forever carefree.

Swaying with the Trees

Up here among the sway and creak,
The trees laugh loud, both strong and meek.
With branches high, they seek to share,
Whimsical secrets blown by air.

A squirrel debates about acorn fashion,
While I'm caught up in their laughter's passion.
Leaves are tittering, rustled by glee,
Who knew that trees could be so free?

Beneath their shade, the world looks bright,
As shadows dance under soft sunlight.
I slip, I trip, but they don't mind,
They're swaying with me, perfectly aligned.

Let's shimmy and groove like we're on a quest,
With branches to hug, we know we're blessed.
As I chuckle, the trees shake their leaves,
In this merry ballet, joy never leaves.

Twilight's Soft Serenade

As daylight fades, stars come out,
I'm here to twirl, sing, and shout.
Fireflies flicker, wearing tiny hats,
Like tiny dancers, buzzing in chats.

The moon joins in, a glowing friend,
Winking slyly, as twilight blends.
Soft whispers float, like giggles in air,
An owl hoots, giving me a scare!

The breeze tickles leaves, laughter so sweet,
While crickets chirp a rhythmic beat.
Under this sky, nonsense does reign,
In twilight's arms, joy is our chain.

So here, I'll sway, with the night's soft grin,
Making mistakes that always win.
With stars dancing bright like some playful cheer,
In this serenade, happiness is clear.

Anchored in the Clouds

Up here, my thoughts take flight,
Each cloud's a fluffy delight.
I dangle my feet, not a care,
To tickle the noses of those down there.

Sipping from mugs of giggly cheer,
Worms in the soil say, "Can we steer?"
My friend the pigeon gives me a wink,
As I ponder the taste of a sky-blue drink.

Clouds are my sofa, so soft and grand,
With a pillow made from a rubber band.
I laugh as thunder rolls in the back,
Jokes whispered between the rain's little crack.

So if you need me, just look up high,
I'm on my perch saying "Why, oh why?"
Life's too short for frowns and strife,
I'll be here living my aerial life.

Breath of the Evening Breeze

The breeze brushes by, gives me a tickle,
Makes me giggle, oh isn't it fickle?
It swirls around like a playful kid,
Pulling my hair and flipping the lid.

Whispers of laughter race through the trees,
Chasing the shadows, trying to tease.
Evening's here, the sun's taking a break,
While crickets are planning their grand, silly shake.

Fireflies dance in a sparkling cheer,
Twinkling stars say, "What's happening here?"
I take a deep breath, feel the night tease,
As I trip over my own two knees!

In this soft glow, all worries are gone,
I'm laughing and playing, the world's my lawn.
Caught in a moment of breezy delight,
Life's funny quirks keep me up every night.

Poetry of the Heights

Up high where the eagles take flight,
I pen funny rhymes, what a sight!
With seagulls joining in on the chat,
We giggle together, isn't that fat?

Writing verses perched on a ledge,
As ants march below, they make their pledge.
To bring me snacks, oh sweet little bugs,
While I lounge with pillows made of hugs.

The wind carries rhymes with a playful dance,
As squirrels stop and stare, lost in a trance.
I'll share my lines with the whole furry crew,
Though they're still plotting to steal my shoe!

So here's to the heights, where laughter flows free,
In this poetic garden, come laugh with me.
From lofty perches, the world seems so small,
Let's call out to nature! Let's giggle and sprawl!

Sipping Sunshine

With a cup of joy, I greet the morn,
Sunshine spills out like corn on the corn.
Each sip a ray, brightening the day,
While my hair stands up, in a goofy display.

Butterflies flutter, critters all cheer,
Having a party, oh dear, oh dear!
I wink at the sun, say, "Give me a break!"
As it beams back, "You're the sunshine flake!"

Sipping on laughter, the nectar of life,
In this bizarre world, I'm free from strife.
Birds chirp in harmony, a symphony sweet,
While ants march by with incredible feet.

So join me, dear friend, in this sunny delight,
We'll sip on the giggles 'til late in the night.
With each blissful gulp, let the fun never cease,
In this vibrant land, we'll sip on our peace.

Laughter in the Clouds

In my little nook so high,
I wave to the birds that fly.
They take a peek, and then they squawk,
While I'm busy sipping my choc-milk rock.

The sun is bright, no shades around,
A seagull lands, I laugh, profound.
He steals my sandwich, oh what a treat,
But I share some crumbs — we're now complete!

In puffy whites that drift and dance,
I throw my worries, give them a chance.
The wind, it tickles my silly grin,
As I lounge in peace, let the giggles begin!

So many layers, my laughter glows,
Can you count the joys my heart owes?
With skies so blue and snacks galore,
It's a cloud of fun, who could ask for more?

Inviting Calm

Sipping tea, I put on a hat,
The flowers giggle, imagine that!
While my cat plots his mighty leap,
I chuckle softly, oh what a sweep!

The clouds are fluffy, a picnic in sight,
I toss my chips, a seagull takes flight.
In a flash, my snack's on the wing,
I laugh aloud, oh what the zing!

A breeze rushes in, shakes the trees,
A squirrel scurries, oh what a tease.
He shakes his tail, gives me a wink,
While I ponder if I need more drink.

The laughter wraps like a warm embrace,
Bringing calm to this silly space.
With gentle smiles and breezy cheer,
In my happy nook, there's nothing to fear!

The Sweet Surrender

With cupcakes stacked and stories shared,
I sink into bliss, no worry bared.
My friends arrive with laughter's ring,
Sugary treats, oh what a fling!

I trip through sprinkles, slip on a bite,
The joyous giggles launch into flight.
In this sugar land, we find delight,
The cake is gone, who planned this plight?

The crumbs tell stories, sweet and wild,
Of silly pranks and a playful child.
With frosting hats, we belt a tune,
Dance like jelly, under the moon!

So here's to laughter, let's raise our glass,
To sugar highs and moments that pass.
In this sweet surrender, we sprinkle bliss,
With every chuckle, it's pure happiness!

Atop the Whispering Heights

Perched on the edge where whispers play,
I'm the queen of silliness, come what may.
The hilltops cheer and the flowers sway,
While I giggle at clouds that drift away.

A kite goes soaring with a mischievous dance,
I tug at its string, oh what a chance!
It loops and spirals, and I'm full of glee,
"Catch me if you can!" says the breeze to me!

With each passing breeze, secrets unfold,
In this whimsical place where dreams are told.
My heart does somersaults, a joyful parade,
As butterflies laugh at the games we've played.

The sun sets low, painting skies in fun,
Stars peek out, oh the night's just begun.
Atop the heights, adorned in delight,
I'll dance with my shadows till morning's light!

Gazing into Dawn's Caress

I sip my tea with a grin,
The sun's peeking through my chin.
Birds chirp tunes that make me laugh,
While squirrels plan their morning gaffe.

The clouds parade in silly shapes,
As shadows dance in joyful scrapes.
My comfy chair, a cloud of ease,
Bouncing thoughts like playful bees.

The garden blooms with colors bright,
While gnomes plot mischief out of sight.
A butterfly winks, flits around,
As if to claim this happy ground.

Morning giggles fill the air,
Chasing away each single care.
With each sip, the world feels light,
In my little nook, pure delight.

Echoes of Peace

I hear the laughter of the breeze,
Tickling leaves like playful tease.
The sun is making shadows sway,
As if to join in on the play.

A dog barks loud with glee and flair,
While ants march off without a care.
The old cat dozes, dreams of fish,
While I dream of a tasty dish.

A pair of socks hangs from a line,
Swapping stories of place and time.
The distant sounds of chirps and skips,
Remind me of my morning dips.

With every whisper of the trees,
I bark back jokes, do as I please.
The echoes bounce, return the fun,
In this calm world, I'm never done.

Twilight's Embrace

The sun dips low, a cheeky grin,
As night sneaks up on sleepy kin.
The crickets start their nightly show,
While stars peek out from cosmic dough.

A firefly winks, a flirt so bold,
While shadows dance, their tales unfold.
I laugh at how the moon's in style,
Draped in clouds and a cheeky smile.

The air's alive with whispering glee,
Every rustle has a secret spree.
Sipping cider, hopes take flight,
As twilight wraps us in its light.

With chuckles shared, the day descends,
Where silly dreams and laughter blend.
In this serenade of night's ballet,
Let joy unfold in merry play.

The Limitless Sky

Up high the kites are soaring free,
Chasing clouds like wild honey bees.
The sky's a canvas, broad and wide,
Where daydreams float and giggles glide.

A flurry of colors, a comical sight,
As paper tails pursue pure delight.
The wind whispers jests, with playful schemes,
While I ponder on my wildly weird dreams.

Each soaring kite like a child's wish,
Dancing high above the squishy fish.
The sun paints smiles all around,
As laughter echoes, joy unbound.

The sky invites us all to play,
In its embrace, we drift away.
With lighter hearts and spirits bright,
We find our bliss in a kite's flight.

A Place for Ascension

Upstairs we cheer with glee,
Where pigeons wink and fly,
My drink spills over me,
  As I reach for the sky.

A cat takes in the scene,
With a judgmental glare,
While I'm lost in a dream,
Floating light as a feather.

Neighbors shout and tease,
They think it's a show,
But we laugh with ease,
When the plants start to grow.

At sunset we all play,
With snack trays piled high,
Turning night into day,
  Oh, the joys of the sky!

The Aerial Sanctuary

We gather round in bliss,
With snacks upon a tray,
Spill a drink with a twist,
And laugh at life's dismay.

A flower pot in place,
It's swaying to the beat,
While the wind plays its race,
And jumbles our feet.

A bird chirps a tune,
To join our silly verse,
Daring us to swoon,
As we laugh and converse.

The stars peek and grin,
Winking down on our fun,
Cherishing our kin,
Under the moonlit run.

A Slice of Infinity

With laughter in the air,
We share our little pie,
While bees try to ensnare,
All the crumbs with a sigh.

A friend trips on the chair,
We all burst into fits,
Our giggles fill the square,
As we watch her antics.

The clouds drift like dreams,
In the realm up so high,
Where joy softly beams,
As the crows pass us by.

In this slice of cheer,
We'll cherish every bite,
For the moments we share,
Sparks a laughter-filled night!

Milestones of Magic

On the edge of delight,
We toast with silly hats,
Making wishes in flight,
With giggles and chitchats.

Our feet dangle down low,
We dare the world to spin,
With each joke and faux show,
Friendship's where we begin.

The stars shine like sprinkles,
As we whisper our dreams,
Sharing giggles and twinkles,
Under moonlit beams.

These moments are our gold,
In our silly parade,
As laughter takes hold,
And joy never fades.

Morning's Sweet Invitation

Sunlight bursts through the pane,
Coffee cups dance a refrain,
A sock in the belly, oh what a sight,
Who knew mornings could be so bright?

Birds outside start their show,
Worms get tangled in a row,
I laugh at my hair, a wild scare,
Doing my best to give them a glare.

Toasts are jumping, can't be still,
Syrup spills, oh what a thrill!
The cat's on the table, claiming his space,
Join the breakfast? Not in this case!

Outside beckons with cheerful cheer,
But cereal knows its partner here,
So let me linger, drink in the light,
Where giggles and crumbs give morning its bite.

The Garden of Solitude

My garden's a jungle, it's out of control,
Weeds in a tango, they're on a roll,
A gnome with a hat, he's losing his flair,
Chasing a squirrel? He just doesn't care!

Sunflowers gossip, all in a row,
"Did you hear what the tulips sow?"
A bee in a bowtie buzzes around,
Trying to dance, but he falls to the ground!

My garden's a riot, where laughter's the weed,
Though my tomato plant's been known to mislead,
It's dressed like a bush, in a greenish disguise,
Sneaking into salads, much to my surprise!

So here in my sanctuary, the whimsy unfurls,
Chasing the critters, twirling with swirls,
I sip on my lemonade, laughing aloud,
In this comical chaos, I'm blissfully proud.

Dreams from the Heights

Up on my roof, I peer at the sky,
Clouds like marshmallows drifting by,
A pigeon's a spy, he's making a call,
While I'm here dreaming of pancakes and all.

The view's rather grand, it's true, you see,
Until a seagull decides to agree,
With a swoosh and a swoop, he claims half my snack,
"Hey, that was my muffin!" - I watch him attack.

Neighbors below in pajamas parade,
While cats do their best to throw shade and evade,
I wave to the folks with a cheeky grin,
On this rooftop of dreams, let the laughter begin!

So here I will stay, surveying my land,
Where whimsy and wonder go hand in hand,
As heights of hilarity lift me with style,
And I savor the sweetness of life with a smile.

Elysian Heights

Perched high above in a world of my own,
Where ice cream clouds build a waffle cone,
Squirrels in tuxedos raise a toast,
To life's little quirks, they're the ones I like most!

The sun plays hopscotch on rooftops below,
While neighbors parade in a bizarre show,
With goats in sunglasses, and dogs in a trance,
Who knew such chaos could lead to a dance?

I toss out some crumbs, watch the antics unfold,
As laughter erupts, let the stories be told,
A breeze full of giggles wraps 'round my face,
In these heights of joy, there's no time to waste!

Here at the summit where jests gently collide,
Life's comedy reigns, it's a glorious ride,
So cuddle your dreams, let them take flight,
In Elysian Heights, everything feels right!

Whispers of Serenity

On the ledge with a view so sweet,
I spy a bird with two left feet.
He wobbles and flutters, what a sight,
As he dances away, oh what delight!

A cat strolls by, looking quite grand,
With a swagger that's simply unplanned.
He claims the sun with a regal pose,
While I sip tea and watch as it goes.

The flowers chat, gossiping with flair,
About a snail who's late for his fair.
He slides along, with dreams in his head,
But at this pace, he'll miss all the bread!

In this haven where laughter blends,
Life is silly, my heart it mends.
With giggles and grins from dawn till night,
I toast to joy, oh what a delight!

Embrace of the Gentle Breeze

The breeze tiptoes, tickling my nose,
As I giggle and pose like a rose.
A squirrel zooms by on a runaway mission,
In search of nuts with great ambition!

A butterfly lands thinking I'm a flower,
I can't help but grin, oh what power!
With wings so bright, it flutters and flaps,
Creating chaos and funny mishaps.

An old man waves, with a hat full of fluff,
His style is unique, but he's full of stuff.
He chats to clouds—they're his best friends,
As joy-filled breezes bring laughter that bends!

Between the giggles and soft, sweet air,
I find moments to dance without a care.
With chuckles and smiles, my spirit's at ease,
In this place where lightness matches the breeze.

Horizon's Peaceful Perch

I perch on high, with legs all akimbo,
As far below, life flows like a limbo.
A dog fetches sticks with a comical bark,
While I sip my juice, feeling quite the spark!

The neighbors argue over a lost shoe,
While I chuckle, thinking 'What could they do?'
The cat next door struts with her crown,
While plotting the downfall of a sleeping frown.

The sunset spills colors, vibrant and wild,
Like a painter's palette, whimsically styled.
As laughter circles from the streets below,
I join the chorus, ready to flow!

In this perch above, where fun intertwines,
With humor that drapes like the finest designs.
Life's little quirks, oh what a surprise,
From my chosen height, I watch the world rise!

Sunlit Escape

A sunbeam pokes my sleepy face,
And I spring up with silly grace.
The world awaits with mirthful tunes,
As I twirl about under bright afternoon moons.

A breeze whispers sweet little jokes,
While I chuckle at clumsy folks.
One trips over nothing, it's such a scene,
He laughs it off—oh, what a routine!

In the garden, daisies are having a ball,
As they invite me to join in their call.
I dance with the petals, all in a whirl,
With a grin that could light up the world!

With shadows that stretch and giggles at play,
The sun dips low, bidding goodbye to the day.
But here, in my corner, the joy still takes shape,
In this sunny escape, oh what a happy landscape!

Symphony of the Open Air

Sitting high amidst the breeze,
My hair's a bird, or so it seems.
With snacks in hand, I spill some treats,
The ants have come, they're keen for eats.

The world below is quite a show,
A cat with pride, a dog in tow.
They prance and dance, no care in sight,
I chuckle loud, what a delight!

The clouds drift by, playing hide and seek,
They need a map, their aim is weak.
I wave and shout, "Oh, come back here!"
They wave a hand, then disappear.

In this treehouse up in the clouds,
I fill my heart, I hum out loud.
Birds tap dance on the window's edge,
I laugh so hard, I break a pledge.

Hues of Quietude

Perched above the bustling street,
My drink spills down, oh what a feat!
A squirrel darts with stealthy grace,
He steals my crumbs, a little ace.

Looking out as people roam,
I shout, "Hey, come back home!"
They turn to stare, then shake their heads,
I guess they think I play instead.

A bird lands near, with a chirp and song,
I hum along, can't get it wrong.
My neighbor's frown is quite amusing,
Maybe my tunes are just confusing?

Butterflies flutter, my friendly spies,
They gossip soft, beneath the skies.
"Oh look at him, oh look at her,"
I sip my tea, and start to stir.

Heartbeats of the Sky

Up here, it's like a circus show,
With folks below, moving to and fro.
A juggler drops his flaming ball,
I cheer him on, what a free-for-all!

A blend of colors fills the street,
A toddler's tantrum can't be beat.
I chuckle loud, it's quite the scene,
Life's a ride, so wild and keen!

Clouds gather round, my furry crew,
They look confused, "What do we do?"
I point below with childlike glee,
"Just wait; I'm ripe for comedy!"

As twilight dances in the west,
I toast to life, I feel so blessed.
A bike goes past, a honk, a scream,
On this cloud, I chase my dream.

Chasing the Dusk

Up above, the world feels trippy,
As sunset paints, I feel so hippy.
A ladder falls, oh what a clatter,
I laugh so hard, what's the matter?

The streetlights blink like fireflies,
I spot a couple, full of sighs.
A little dog, with gusto barks,
He chases shadows, leaves his marks.

The sky's ablaze, pink and orange hues,
I hear the gossip, sipping brews.
"Did you see her in those shoes?"
I snicker soft, have they no clues?

As night unfolds its velvet cloak,
I weave my dreams with every stroke.
The world below fades into night,
From up here, it feels just right!

Whispers of the Wind

A breeze so lively, tickles the ear,
Chasing my thoughts like a mischievous deer.
Laughter erupts as I swat at the flies,
Nature's own prankster under bright blue skies.

The trees wave hello, in a jolly old dance,
Spinning their leaves in a playful romance.
I join in the fun, twirling about,
While squirrels gossip, there's never a doubt.

Butterflies flutter, adorned in their best,
Critiquing my dance, they think it's a jest.
I bow with flair, with a grin on my face,
Admit it, you loved that embarrassing grace!

As shadows grow long and the sun dips away,
The whispers grow louder, in the twilight's play.
With chuckles from daisies, and smirks from the pines,
I embrace their humor, life's quirks intertwine.

Essence of Elevated Calm

Up here on my perch, the world feels so small,
Clouds parade by, oh, how I sprawl!
Tea in my hand, biscuits just right,
Daydreams and giggles take flight like a kite.

With every soft sip, I can't help but grin,
Imagining squirrels planning a spin.
As joys float around in a buttery swirl,
My chair leans back, into laughter I whirl.

The birds hold a concert, oh what a scene,
Their tunes are a mix of sweet and obscene.
A tune here, a chirp there, they wail with glee,
Who knew nature's choir was all about me?

The sun turns to gold, painting skies with delight,
Even the shadows join in on this light.
On this crest of bliss, jokes tumble and blend,
I lift up my cup, to a sky that won't end!

The Lull of the Stars

Underneath the glitter, the jokes are on high,
Stars wink and giggle, as they float by.
They whisper of wishes that fell all around,
Raining down chuckles, the silliest sound.

A comet zooms past, what a clumsy old guy,
With his tail all a-flutter, oh me, oh my!
The moon plays the jester, with shadows it casts,
Turning my dreams into fanciful blasts.

Each twinkle a chuckle, each glow a soft tease,
As laughter echoes through the cosmos with ease.
I join the parade, with pajamas on tight,
Dancing with fireflies, a magical sight!

So here in the night, as the world seems so quaint,
I chuckle with stars, and a giggler, a saint.
In this cavalcade of celestial mirth,
I revel in joy, for all it is worth.

Mornings on the Edge

Awake to the chirps, oh what a delight,
The sun plays peekaboo, saying, 'Goodnight!'
With coffee in hand, I'm ready to chat,
But the cat just yawns and sprawls out flat.

Socks mismatched, what a lovely design,
I claim it's a trend, it's divine and just fine!
The toast jumps up, startled and brave,
While I ponder the day, a whimsical wave.

The flowers burst in laughter, oh what a show,
Tickled by dew drops that sparkle and glow.
I join them with giggles, a chorus in bloom,
As the humor of mornings fills every room.

With each silly moment, I jump in the air,
Bounding with joy, like I haven't a care.
On this edge filled with chuckles, I let out a sigh,
Another day begins, under a bright, peeking sky!

Silhouettes at Sundown

As shadows dance on the ground,
The sun plays tricks all around.
With quirky shapes in the light,
We laugh till the stars are in sight.

A cat poses like a king,
While birds tease with their winged fling.
We mimic their chirps all in fun,
Turns out, we're the real silly ones.

Neighbors peek through their blinds,
Wondering what our antics find.
With goofy grins and happy shouts,
The night wears off our silly doubts.

As dusk spills colors, so bright,
We toast to laughter, pure delight.
Let's keep the giggles in play,
And watch shadows make their way.

Notes of Infinity

Whistling tunes of the absurd,
Each note floats like a clumsy bird.
We try to catch them in the air,
But they vanish, that's only fair.

The moon joins in our little song,
With echoes that go on too long.
Our voices blend, a silly choir,
Oh, how we giggle and conspire.

With every laugh, a thought appears,
Of cosmic pizza and space pies, cheers!
We ponder life beyond the stars,
With macaroni, moonlit jars.

Each note that flutters in the breeze,
Sprinkles joy like dandelion seeds.
In this symphony of good cheer,
We find infinity's giggle near.

The Summit's Secret

At the peak where clouds float high,
We whispered secrets to the sky.
With each gust of wind, a prank,
Made us laugh till we couldn't thank.

We learned the summit's little trick,
To balance rocks, quick and slick.
But in our haste, rocks tumbled down,
Rolling like a tiny clown.

With funny hats made of leaves,
We giggled loud and shared our eves.
The mountain echoed with our cheer,
All the while, the squirrels peeked near.

As sunset spread its golden gown,
We danced like fools, no trace of frown.
At the summit's point, our hearts were free,
The secret joy of light and glee.

Skylines of Serenity

With crayons drawing the skyline bright,
We scribble clouds, a wondrous sight.
A penguin wears a tiny hat,
While dogs float by on a silver mat.

Beneath the twilight's shiny glow,
We huddle close in a silly row.
Sharing stories of our batty day,
What wrong goes right in a fun way?

Here, a tall building sways and leans,
A sight that's worthy of silly scenes.
We cheer for all the quirky sights,
As giggles fill these dreamy nights.

The skyline blinks like a starry eye,
Winking at us with secrets nigh.
In this world where laughter rings,
Blissful joy in the oddest things.

A Haven Above the Ground

In a perch where I munch, high in the sky,
Neighbors wonder who's that guy,
Eating snacks with a laugh and a wave,
As seagulls plot and misbehave.

Below, the world is a bustling show,
I watch with glee, the highs and the lows.
A cat on a leash, a dog in a hat,
Life's a circus, and I'm loving that!

With my feet dangling, I sip on my tea,
Making faces at folks — oh, what a spree!
A cloud-shaped throne, where giggles reside,
Here in my kingdom, silliness is wide!

Oh, the dreams I weave in my lofty retreat,
Where laughter's a language, oh, so sweet.
The sun sets slowly, spilling out gold,
And here I stay, forever bold!

The Calm Between Clouds

Bouncing between laugh and playful sigh,
Waves of whimsy, like kites flying high.
Squinting my eyes at the playful jest,
Finding joy in the cozy nest.

A bird with a hat, a squirrel with flair,
Whispering secrets only clouds share.
Juggling puns like those orange peels,
In this abode where happiness reels.

I sip on sunshine, dance in delight,
Twirl to the music of day into night.
Where each little giggle takes off on a trip,
Floating with dreams on an airy slip.

Here I concoct laughter's sweet brew,
With a sprinkle of mischief and maybe some glue.
A moment of joy, a slice of the fun,
In this magical place, forever rerun!

Treading on Air

Up here I float, with a wink and a grin,
Kittens doing ballet, where do I begin?
A dance on the edge with marshmallow toes,
My audience squawks, oh, how the joy grows!

Bubbles are popping, they tickle my nose,
Frolicsome dreams spraying glittering prose.
With lemonade rivers and candy cane waves,
This silly sweet world, oh, how it behaves!

Tickling clouds while I juggle some dreams,
Laughter and giggles like soft glitter screams.
Over the roof, with no worry or care,
Who knew that joy felt just like—treading air?

Breezy adventures wrapped in a bow,
Every chuckle a seed we sow.
I'll bounce between wonders till stars start to gleam,
In this frothy escape, life's a funny dream!

Cascade of Daydreams

Swinging through thoughts like a breeze with a twirl,
Painting the sky with giggles that swirl.
Banana peels scattered, as I take a break,
Whimsical wonders with every mistake.

A waterfall of chuckles cascades from above,
Where silly ideas give birth to love.
The clouds are my friends, they've got jokes to share,
Cracking me up with their fluff and their flair.

Napkins become capes, I wear them with pride,
Dancing with shadows, the silliness slide.
Tickled by breezes, oh what a fate,
This twisty little space where joy generates!

As I brew up a storm of mirth and of light,
Every moment's a chance, a whimsical flight.
And when night falls, we'll just laugh some more,
In the quiet of laughter, happiness soars!

The View from Tranquility

In pajamas with a cup of tea,
I ponder life so blissfully.
Birds gossip while I chill at noon,
Who knew that fluff could be a tune?

Sunshine filters through the trees,
A dance of shadows in the breeze.
I wave at squirrels who act so grand,
They think they rule this patch of land.

Stray clouds float by without a clue,
Are they lost, or just passing through?
I snicker as they drift away,
Smart move, I'd rather nap than play.

In this haven, laughter roams,
With silly thoughts, I build my homes.
Where fun meets the fluff of dreams so bright,
Here's where my heart feels truly light.

Serenity's Perch

Perched above the world so high,
I watch my neighbors try to fly.
Their garden gnomes stare back at me,
As if they hold a secret spree.

With birds as jesters, jesting free,
They squawk with glee and flit with glee.
I feel like royalty in my chair,
Beneath the laughter, I've found my heir.

The cat declares it's time to nap,
While butterflies dance on a map.
They spin in circles, such a sight,
My heart can't help but feel delight.

I sip my drink, oh what a day,
Life's little quirks all come to play.
In my sanctuary of cheer,
It's the best place to be, I cheer!

Moments of Solitude

In solitude, I find the best,
My thoughts in chaos take a rest.
A bird drops by, a feathery friend,
Who states he's only here to lend.

He judges me for my silly ways,
As I wear my mismatched socks for days.
With laughter bubbling just below,
He tells me, "Hey, why not steal the show?"

So, I put on a hat, quite absurd,
And give a speech as if I've heard.
The wind applauds with playful sighs,
While gnomes nod wisely, oh so wise.

Here in the clouds of quiet thought,
Where nonsense blooms and smiles are caught.
In moments quaint, I find my fun,
Oh, solitude, you're my number one!

Where Sky Meets Heart

Up where the sky winks at my soul,
And fluffy clouds take on a role.
They float like marshmallows in my mind,
While below, the world's in a dance unaligned.

I see a kite with dreams so bold,
Tangled in a tree, now that's pure gold.
Laughter escapes as it flaps with glee,
"Oh my, that's not where you should be!"

The sun-warmed air invites a jest,
While butterflies wear their finest vest.
They gossip in whispers, so very sly,
While I chuckle at clouds that seem to cry.

In this whimsical space where giggles start,
Where even the breeze plays a comical part.
My heart swells with joy, a whimsical dart,
Finding joy in solace, where sky meets heart.

Nestled in the Clouds

Up high where the pigeons graze,
I sip my drink, gaze in a daze.
My feet dangle, wind in my hair,
Are those clouds or just cotton candy flair?

A squirrel winks, he's stealing my fries,
While bees plot a heist; such silly spies.
I dance with the sun, no care in the world,
Until the wind gives my umbrella a twirl.

Laughter drips from the sky like rain,
As my hat takes off, what a crazy train!
Joy rocket-launches with each gusty blow,
In this sky-high playground where giggles grow.

So let's toast to the view, it's better than gold,
Life's a circus, and I'm just the bold.
With a splash of confetti, we conquer the breeze,
In this cloud-top haven, we do as we please.

Unfurling Moments

Up here where the world looks small,
Tickling the clouds, I hear their call.
A napkin sails by, seeks sweet freedom,
It's a comedy show in cloudy kingdom.

I juggle my snacks, a great ballerina,
But they roll away like a rogue patina.
With squirrels as critics, I laugh and I grin,
Munching on popcorn—I'm ready to win!

They cheer as I spill my drink over the rail,
Running off like a mouse, oh dear, what a fail!
But laughter's the remedy, joy's in the air,
At this sky-high party, without any care.

So here's to the mishaps, the giggles galore,
With each silly moment, I simply want more.
Unfurling my heart, I let out a tune,
Dancing with clouds, beneath the bright moon.

Table for One with the Sky

The table's set high with a view that's divine,
I dine on dreams, and a pinch of sunshine.
A slice of the moon, served with old stars,
And whispers of laughter from planets afar.

My napkin flies off, it's a party today,
As birds dance around in a wobbly ballet.
Peering at traffic, I giggle with glee,
What's funnier than humans—oh, wait, it's me!

With tea brewed from giggles, I sip and I ponder,
How nature provides quite the slapstick wonder.
The sun trips on clouds, with a radiant flare,
Illuminating moments, through the light, we share.

So here's to my table, where skies bring delight,
With every silly slip, it feels oh-so-right.
A toast to the cosmos, with laughter we fry,
For this gathering up here, is a treat for the sky.

The Quiet Constellation

A hush in the sparkles of cosmic delight,
As stars occasionally sneeze, what a sight!
They twinkle and shake, a dazzling display,
Who knew they had allergies? Oh, what a play!

In the still of the night, I'm counting my friends,
The giggling meteors zoom 'round the bends.
With laughter and whispers, they're plotting a show,
"Let's star in a comedy!" they gleefully crow.

The moon pops in, with a wink and a grin,
"Join me for jokes, let the fun now begin!"
I chuckle and chatter amidst twinkling lights,
Their humor shines brighter than all city nights.

So here in the quiet, where laughter takes flight,
I cuddle with stardust, blissful and bright.
In this cosmic realm where the stillness is loud,
We gather together, a shimmering crowd.

Gathering of Gentle Sighs

On the ledge, we laugh and play,
Counting clouds that drift away.
Birds gossip with a chirpy cheer,
While we munch on snacks right here.

Joyful jests bounce through the air,
Spilling secrets without a care.
The breeze carries our giggles by,
As butterflies attempt to fly.

With feet hanging over the side,
We watch silly squirrels collide.
Nature calls with a funny peek,
Atop this perch, we're truly unique.

So let the sunbeam tickle our toes,
As we share tales nobody knows.
In this light-hearted, happy place,
Friendship blooms at a comical pace.

Freedom's Elevated Refuge

Perched high above in our fun spot,
With lemonade and a pizza lot.
The world below is noisy and loud,
Here we giggle, free and proud.

From our heights, the city is small,
While we invent our own waterfall.
Just a sip, and we're flying high,
Our laughter floats up to the sky.

Unseen acrobats tumble and dance,
In our heads, we give them a chance.
A neighborhood cat joins the scene,
With its antics, it's a great meme.

As shadows stretch at the day's end,
We toast to life with every friend.
In this haven, joy's really the key,
Where quirks and quirks blend seamlessly.

Whispers of Serenity

In the quiet, we share a glance,
As an ant performs a funny dance.
The flowers nod in time with glee,
While we sip tea, just you and me.

Raindrops chase the wind's sharp tune,
As we trade stories with the moon.
Each chuckle floats in soft echoes,
As giggles bloom like autumn's rose.

A broomstick is a flying steed,
With wild imaginations to feed.
We soar above the rooftops wide,
In our minds, oh what a ride!

Embraced by dusk's gentle sigh,
The stars peek in, like they're shy.
With whispers soft, we end the day,
In this serenity, we'll always stay.

Dreams Above the Edge

Up here we plot a daring sky,
With clouds as pillows, oh so high.
Rooftop dreams of cakes and pies,
With powdered sugar from our eyes.

We balance on the edge of fun,
Chasing sunsets, one by one.
Hats that twirl on heads askew,
Welcomed laughter, bright and new.

The moon joins in our playful fight,
Casting shadows like daylight.
As the stars wink down with grace,
We find magic in this space.

So here's to nights that never end,
Where whimsy dances, round each bend.
In our sanctuary, silly and bright,
We dream of dreams in pure delight.

www.ingramcontent.com/pod-product-compliance
Lightning Source LLC
Chambersburg PA
CBHW070307120526
44590CB00017B/2586